Bim, the
Very Special Bear

Frances Li

Illustrated by J

HODDER AND STOUGHTON
LONDON SYDNEY AUCKLAND TORONTO

This book is dedicated to all children, grandmas, and brave captains.

British Library Cataloguing in Publication Data

Lindsay, Frances
   Bim, the very special bear.
   I. Title   II. Cope, Jane
   823'.914[J]   PZ7

   ISBN 0-340-40808-1

Published by Hodder and Stoughton Children's Books, a division of Hodder and Stoughton Ltd, Mill Road, Dunton Green, Sevenoaks, Kent TN13 2YJ

Photoset by Rowland Phototypesetting Ltd, Bury St Edmunds, Suffolk

Printed in Great Britain by St Edmundsbury Press Ltd, Bury St Edmunds, Suffolk

Bim, the Very Special Bear

Also by Frances Lindsay

In the Hopscotch series
THE HALF–PRICE BEAR

In the Leapfrog series
MR BITS AND PIECES
BITS AND PIECES SOLVES A MYSTERY
BITS AND PIECES AND THE SMUGGLERS

Loppy Ears Adventures
THE CIRCUS TREAT
THE CLEVER CLUE
THE SUPER SECRET
THE TREASURE HUNT

Bim was pleased when Toby said they
were going to Grandma for a holiday. 'I
like her. She gave me a peppermint toffee
the other day.'

'That's Grandma-down-the-road.
We're going to Grandma-at-the-seaside.
She's nice too.'

'You are lucky to have two Grandmas.
I haven't got one,' Bim said sadly.

'Never mind. You've got me,' said Toby and he gave the little koala a big hug. He had known Bim was a Very Special Bear the moment he saw him in Mr Totty's toy shop, and had bought him instead of a police car. It did not seem the least bit strange to find that Bim could talk, but only Toby and his sisters Jemma and Beth knew that. No one else knew that Bim was magic.

After breakfast they all went to the toy shop. Mr Totty was pleased to see them, especially Bim. He often wished he had never sold the little koala.

Bim was delighted when Toby and the girls bought him a little red bucket and spade. 'Thank you very much. I've never had such a lovely present before,' he said.

Mr Totty turned pale. 'I almost thought I heard him say thank you,' he whispered.

'I'm sure he would if he could,' said Toby and, calling goodbye, they all left the shop.

Early next morning Mum, Dad, Bim and the children set off in the car to the seaside and sang jolly songs and played 'I-Spy' all the way.

Grandma was as nice as Toby had said she would be and her little home, with its lopsided roof and crooked chimney pot, looked like a cottage in a fairy tale.

In the garden was a caravan where the children were to sleep. 'It's more fun out here. We can have feasts whenever we like,' Jemma said.

'And tell each other stories,' Beth added.

Inside the caravan were two bunks and a table which turned into a bed. 'Bim and I will sleep in the top bunk, Jemma. You and Beth can take it in turn to sleep in the bottom one.'

'Will there be room in the bunk for my bucket and spade?' Bim asked.

Toby laughed. 'It'll be all right in the garden, Bim.'

'I don't want it to get dirty.'

'It will soon get dirty when you start building sandcastles.'

Grandma came into the caravan. 'I have a surprise for you children,' she said. 'Auntie Sue and cousin James are coming to stay.'

'Cousin James!'* The children stared at her in dismay and Grandma said quickly, 'I know he used to be a naughty boy but I'm sure he's better now.'

'We don't want nasty, horrid James in the caravan with us. He's a spiteful boy,' Jemma cried.

'He won't be in the caravan with you. He'll sleep in the cottage. Please be nice to him.'

The children looked at each other. 'All right, Grandma,' said Toby. 'We'll try.'

'If *he's* nice to *us*,' said Beth.

'Thank you, my dears,' said Grandma, but as she hurried away Jemma couldn't help whispering, 'He won't be. He'll spoil everything.'

I won't let him, Bim thought.

After dinner, Dad went home leaving Mum with the children, who could not wait to go on the beach.

* See *The Half-Price Bear*

'You'd better stay here, Bim,' said
Toby.

'I don't want to. I want to go with you
and build a great big sandcastle.'

'But people will know you're not a toy
bear if they see you doing that, and
someone may try to steal you. You'll be
safer keeping Beakie company.'

'Who's Beakie?'

'Grandma's parrot.'

As soon as everyone had gone to the beach, Bim went into the cottage. He had been longing to explore it ever since Toby had told him about Grandma's home. He wanted to sit in the chimney corner that Toby called an inglenook and look up the chimney to see the sky. Toby said it could only be done when the fire was not alight.

There was no fire today and Bim was able to look right up the chimney and see the sky. 'It's big enough for the fattest Father Christmas to come down,' he exclaimed.

'Naughty boy! Naughty boy!' a voice suddenly screeched at him. It was Beakie.

Bim giggled. 'Naughty yourself,' he said and sat in a rocking-chair.

'Naughty boy!' Beakie screamed again and gave such a loud squawk that the little bear nearly fell off the chair with fright. 'Be quiet!' he shouted but he only succeeded in making the parrot shriek even louder. Bim could bear it no longer.

He went out of the room, up a twisty
staircase, then climbed rickety steps into
the attic. There, in the middle of piles of
boxes and cases, sat an old teddy bear. He
wore a bandage round his head, a patch
over one eye and his right arm was in a
sling.

Bim crept up to him. 'Are you awake?'
he whispered.

The bear opened his good eye and
glared at Bim. 'No, I'm not! Can't you
see I'm asleep?' he snapped.

'I'm sorry. I didn't mean to disturb
you.'

'H'm! I thought it was that boy James. He never leaves me in peace. Always wants to pull me about. I'm too old for that.' He peered at Bim. 'Who are you?'

'I'm Bim – Toby's bear.'

'Koalas aren't bears.'

'I am. I'm a special kind of bear.'

'And I'm Captain Tim, the bravest bear you'll ever meet. I lost my eye fighting pirates when I was in the Navy.'

'Pirates! How awful. Weren't you frightened?'

'Of course I wasn't. Captains are never frightened.'

'Was that when you hurt your head?'

'No. That was when I was in the Air Force. I was shot down by the enemy; and I lost my arm when I was in the Army. They sewed it back but it's never been much good.' He yawned and closed his eyes. 'I'll tell you more about it another day.'

Bim crept downstairs into the garden. Last night's rain had left puddles on the path and he had fun jumping in them and making big splashes until he heard a car drawing up and James shouting, 'Hi Gran. I want . . .'

Bim did not wait to hear more. He raced back into the cottage and burst into the attic. Captain Tim frowned. 'That's not the way to enter a room, young Bim.

I thought you had better manners than that.'

'Sorry, Captain Tim, but there's bad news. Cousin James has come. We must hide.'

The brave Captain clambered to his feet. 'It's action stations, my lad. The enemy must be defeated. We will withdraw to our positions.'

'We must hide, Captain Tim. That's what we must do.'

Captain Tim seemed to crumple. 'There's nowhere we *can* hide. It won't take James long to find us. He knows every corner of this attic.'

'Then we must stop him from getting in.'

'How can we do that?'

'We'll lock the door.'

'We can't reach the key.'

'We can if I stand on your shoulders.'

Captain Tim laughed and helped Bim up but the key was still out of reach. The little bear knew then it was time to use his magic. He whispered a secret word and the key turned in the lock, just as James ran up the stairs. He rattled the handle noisily but the door was shut fast and he hurled himself against it, kicking it angrily when it would not open.

'What are you doing, making all that noise? Come down at once!' Grandma called.

'I want to see that old bear.'

'I've told you before to leave him alone. You've done quite enough damage to him already.'

'I only want to look at him.'

'Come down at once!'

James knew that Grandma meant what she said but he could not resist a last kick at the door. It stood as firm as a rock and, defeated, he went downstairs.

Captain Tim drew himself up. 'Well done, Bim. The enemy has retreated and we are in command. I shall recommend you for a decoration – when I've had a little nap of course.'

He was asleep immediately and as Bim crept downstairs he heard Grandma scolding James's mother. 'He's tired from the long journey,' she answered. 'He's a good boy really.'

'He's a naughty boy, Sue, you know he is. It's your silly fault for spoiling him.'

Bim did not wait to hear more, but ran out into the garden. A moment later James came out too and, because he was not looking where he was going, he ran BANG! into a tree . . .

The next thing he knew he was in a beautiful garden and a jolly-looking koala bear was saying, 'There's lots to see in the Land of Make Believe.'

James stared across the garden and saw dolls and teddy bears of all descriptions, lying in beds or sitting in chairs. Some had bandages round their heads; others had lost an arm, or a leg or an eye. A toy soldier was hobbling about on crutches whilst another pushed himself along in a wheelchair. Despite their injuries they looked happy.

The koala spoke again. 'These poor toys have been ill-treated by spiteful children and rescued from dustbins and rubbish heaps. They are looked after by toys from good homes where boys and girls know how to treat them.'

James had never felt so ashamed. He, too, had treated toys badly, especially Grandma's old teddy bear. He hung his head. 'I'm sorry. I won't do it again,' he whispered. Then, looking into the distance, he saw a wonderful castle with golden turrets and silver fountains. 'If I'm good can I come here again?' he asked eagerly.

Bim smiled. 'Children can go anywhere if they use their imagination, James . . . '

The boy rubbed his eyes and Grandma, coming into the garden, saw him sitting under the apple tree, a dazed look on his face.

'Are you all right?' she asked.

Bewildered, the boy slowly stood up. The koala bear and Toy's Rest Home had disappeared. He was back in Grandma's garden. Yet he could not believe it had all been a dream. 'I'm sorry I was naughty, Gran,' he said.

Grandma smiled. 'That's what I've been waiting to hear,' she answered and gave him a hug.

Although James grumbled because he was
not allowed to sleep in the caravan, he
was good for the next few days.
(Grandma feared he was sickening for
something.) However, one morning he
could not resist teasing the parrot.
'Naughty boy! Naughty boy!' Beakie
shrieked.

'Shut up or I'll pull out your feathers,'
James shouted rudely. No sooner had he
said it than it seemed a good idea, and he
opened the cage.

'You're not very good at keeping promises, are you?' said a voice.

James stared unbelievingly at the toy bear sitting in the rocking-chair.

'He was going to pull out my feathers,' Beakie squawked.

'I know he was, and after all he promised,' said Bim.

James blushed. 'I . . . I wasn't g...going to hurt him,' he stammered. 'I...I was trying to be good.'

'You must try harder,' said Bim, and at once became a silent toy again. Puzzled, James stared at the little bear and then ran out of the room, wondering if he had imagined what he had heard or whether his conscience had been reminding him of his promise.

James's resolution to be good lasted longer than it had before, and Bim was able to spend more time listening to Captain Tim's wonderful stories.

One day the old bear told him about the marvellous adventure he had had when he flew in the first spacecraft. 'I was a Very Special Adviser,' he said. 'No one except me knew I was there. It was all very hush-hush . . . very secret.' Then, opening his good eye wider, he said proudly, 'We Very Special Bears can do all manner of things if we put our minds to it.'

'Of course we can,' said Bim. He looked out of the attic window to the beach where Toby was swimming and Beth and Jemma were collecting shells. As usual, James was playing by himself. It's time those children became friends, thought Bim.

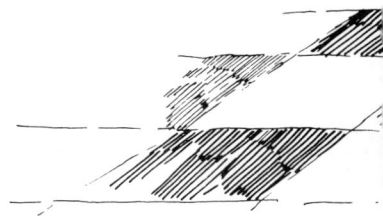

The next morning, on the way to the beach, James tripped on some stone steps and hurt his face. He felt like crying, until he heard a man say what a brave little boy he was. It made him swallow his tears and pretend he had not been hurt. Grandma bathed his bruises and put ice-cubes on his nose to stop it bleeding, but it was still swollen the next morning, and he felt miserable.

'You'd better not go to the beach today but stay quietly in the garden, James. I'll read you a story when I've finished my jobs,' Grandma promised.

'I want to stay in the garden and play with James,' said Beth. 'We can play hospitals and I'll be the nurse.'

It was the first time anyone had wanted
to play with James for a long time, and
suddenly he felt happy.

Grandma gave Beth some bandages and
tied a big handkerchief round her head
and another round her waist. 'Now you
look like a nurse,' she said.

Beth bandaged James's arms and legs
until he could hardly move. He soon said
he felt better, so she let him be the doctor
and her dolls the patients and they played
happily all the morning.

On the last day of the holiday the children had a party in the beach hut and played cricket until the sun went down. James had never been so nice or so friendly, and Toby and the girls said he could sleep in the caravan with them and they would tell each other stories.

Toby's was about a wicked monster. It frightened Beth, so Jemma told a funny story about a witch who could not make her spells work because she did silly things.

Beth's story was about a kind and beautiful fairy called Beth. It made them laugh and they teased her for calling the fairy Beth.

Then it was James's turn. He thought hard for a moment and said, 'It's a story about a kind bear, only it's . . . '

'You must begin at the beginning,' Jemma interrupted.

'Say once upon a time,' Beth said helpfully.

'Well, once upon a time there was a kind bear and a naughty boy . . . only he didn't mean to be naughty . . . '

'What was his name?' Toby asked.

James went red. 'He hasn't got a name . . . '

'He must have; everyone has a name.'

'This boy hasn't . . . '

'Don't interrupt, Toby! Oh, do get on with it, James,' said Jemma.

'Well, this kind bear looked after dolls and bears and things that have, I mean had, been hurt by horrid girls and boys. He . . . he rescued them and took them to a lovely place to get better.'

Bim, sitting on the top bunk, winked at
Toby. A broad grin crossed Toby's face
and he held up the little koala. 'Is the bear
like Bim?' he asked.

James looked up. 'No. That's a toy
bear. The one I'm telling you about was, I
mean is, a real bear.'

'He sounds like a magic bear to me,'
said Jemma.

'I expect he is,' Beth agreed. The children looked knowingly at each other. 'Go on with the story, James,' urged Jemma.

'There isn't any more,' he answered.

'What happened to the naughty boy?' asked Jemma.

'Well, he became good because he saw how badly the poor toys had been treated,' said James.

'Then everyone lived happily ever after,' finished Beth.

'Good. Now we can have our feast,' said Jemma.

There was just time for crisps, dolly-mixtures and sultanas before they went to sleep.

'Must we clean our teeth again?' Beth asked.

'We're excused when we have a feast,' said Jemma.

Bim, hiding in the top bunk, whispered, 'It was very nice, Toby – the things you gave me – but I would have liked a peppermint toffee.'

Toby felt under the pillow and brought out a toffee covered in fluff. 'It's been in my pocket so it's a bit dirty, Bim, but you can have it if you like.'

'Thank you, Toby. It's only clean dirt in your pocket.' Bim popped the toffee into his mouth and chewed happily, thinking as he had so often done before how much nicer sausages would taste if they were made of peppermint.

Before he went home, James thanked
Grandma for a lovely holiday.

'You've been a very good boy,' she
said.

'I know I have, Gran,' said James, who
had discovered how much nicer everyone
and everything was when HE was being
good. He had completely forgotten the
help he had had from the koala bear. That
had all been a dream.

Whilst the girls were saying goodbye to Grandma, Toby went in search of Bim and found him in the attic. 'What are you doing, Bim? We're ready to go.'

'I'm saying goodbye to Captain Tim.'

Toby looked at the old bear and laughed. 'You mean old Timothy?'

'I mean Captain Tim, the bravest bear in the Navy, the Army and the Air Force. Did you know he lost his eye fighting pirates?'

'Who told you that?'

'He did.'

Toby took Bim downstairs to say goodbye to Grandma and thank her for having them and, while Dad was piling the luggage into the car, Toby told Bim that the old bear was a fibber. 'He's never been in the Navy, the Army or the Air Force. He's always lived with Grandma. James poked his eye out. He nearly pulled old Timothy's head off too.'

Bim longed to tell Toby of the magic Very Special Bears have, the magic that had given Captain Tim so many exciting adventures, but all he said was, 'I don't think he meant to fib.'

Toby hugged his kind-hearted little bear. 'I don't suppose he did, either . . . '

Far away from Mr Totty's toy shop, a magician was busy making toys. As he worked he sang:

'Which lucky child shall I please today
What special toy shall I make?
A boat or a car, a kite that flies far,
A dog that can walk, a doll that will talk,
An engine, a train, a tank or a plane,
A garage, a house, a cat or a mouse?
All special toys to please girls and boys . . .'

A large bird flew on to the magician's shoulder. 'Make a bear – a very special bear,' he cawed.

The magician looked thoughtful. 'I once made a most unusual bear. The finest you ever did see.'

'Make another like it. Make another like it!'

'I could never do that.'

'Why not? Why not?'

'Because I could only make one half as good and a half as good bear is no good at all,' said the magician.